49 DAYS OF FASTING AND PRAYERS
for
YEAR 2021 AD
EXHORTATION AND PRAYERS
for
RIGHTEOUSNESS IN CHRIST
(Time for me to receive big dreams and make great achievements in Christ)

2021 is THE YEAR OF THE RIGHTEOUSNESS OF CHRIST IN MY LIFE. This year I begin to receive from the Holy Spirit, enlargement of the capacity of my heart to dream big and make great divine achievements in my life, health, career, ministry, marriage, home, children, finance, etc. Our Church is established in righteousness and flourishing in the gospel of Christ. In Jesus Name.

2021 is THE YEAR OF THE RIGHTEOUSNESS OF CHRIST IN MY LIFE
(Psalm 112:1-10; Isaiah 54:11-17; Romans 5:17-21; 2 Corinthians 5:14-21; Titus 3:3-7)

CHRISTIAN FOUNDATIONS (CHRISFO)
SALVATION HOUSE,
Off Pipeline Road, Baale Akinosi, Ajuwon-Akute
christianfoundations88@yahoo.com
www.chrisfo.org

EXHORTATION & PRAYER POINTS
For
RIGHTEOUSNESS IN CHRIST

Contents

OPERATION
HOLINESS &
RIGHTEOUSNESS

TUE. DEC. 1 '20 - SUN. FEB. 7, '21

Prophetic Teachings
Sunday // 9am

Prophetic Prayers
Tuesdays // 6pm

Thanksgiving
Ministrations
Fridays // 10pm

 Chapel of Beauty & Glory
SALVATION HOUSE ESTATE,
Baale Akinosi, Ajuwon - Akute

Join us LIVE ON

mixlr.com/chrisfo

Christian Foundations CHRISFO

ChristianFoundations

Christian Foundations-CHRISFO

 **CHRISTIAN FOUNDATIONS
MISSIONARY CHURCH (CFMC)**
www.chrisfo.org

MARRIAGE ● ● ● ●
ENRICHMENT 2021
singles · married · single parents
Wed Mar 31 - Mon. April 5

Chapel of Beauty & Glory
SALVATION HOUSE ESTATE,
Baale Akinosi, Ajuwon - Akute
Join us LIVE ON
mixlr.com/chrisfo
Christian Foundations CHRISFO
ChristianFoundations
Christian Foundations-CHRISFO

CHRISTIAN FOUNDATIONS
MISSIONARY CHURCH (CFMC)

LETTER FROM THE PASTOR

Friday. January 1, 2021

Dearly Beloved,

THE YEAR OF RIGHTEOUSNESS IN CHRIST

For most of us who came into Christ through the so-called Holiness Movement, the concept of righteousness connotes rigorous self-efforts to obey God's written commands as we interpret them from the Bible. Unfortunately, that is an impossible task because the Bible itself says that those laws we were striving to obey, were made to prove us guilty and NOT to "justify or make us righteous"

"Now we know that whatever the law says, it says to those who are under the law, that every mouth may be stopped, and all the world may become guilty before God. Therefore by the deeds of the law no flesh will be justified in His sight, for by the law is the

knowledge of sin. But now the righteousness of God apart from the law is revealed, being witnessed by the Law and the Prophets" Rom. 3:19-22

The additional burden of that type of concept of righteousness includes

i.   Frustrating legalism that tended to lead some to give up their faith or adopt a self-deceiving hypocritical attitude to life.

ii.   This, in my opinion, is the reason for the judgemental, bitter and "holier than thou" approach to others;

iii.   It might sometimes appear like bitter-envy against the others who profess the same faith and inheritance in Christ with us, while they maintain free minded, bold and more productive attitude to life.

iv.   Legalism could be so suffocating, burdensome and life-draining

v.   So many people from such a background are usually limited in ambition, pursuit and fulfilment in many areas of life in spite of their apparent God-given potentials.

Of Course, there is the other extreme side of those who abuse the gift of righteousness in Christ as license to gratify the lusts of the flesh, etc. To them, the gift of righteousness to Christians by faith exempts them from the responsibility to cultivate the life-transforming fellowship of the Holy Spirit in the basic means of grace in their God-required pursuit of practical righteousness and holiness unto the LORD. They decide to ignore scriptures like:

"What shall we say then? Shall we continue in sin that grace may abound? Certainly not! How shall we who died to sin live any longer in it? Or do you not know that as many of us as were baptized into Christ Jesus were baptized into His death? Therefore we were buried with Him through baptism into death, that just as Christ was raised from the dead by the glory of the Father, even so we also should walk in newness of life." Romans 6:1-4

"Little children, let no one deceive you. He who practices righteousness is righteous, just as He is righteous. He who sins is of the devil, for the devil has sinned from the beginning. For this purpose the Son of God was manifested, that He might destroy the works of the devil. Whoever has been born of God does not sin, for His seed remains in him; and he cannot sin, because he has been born of God." 1 John 3:7-9

"But even to this day, when Moses is read, a veil lies on their heart. Nevertheless when one turns to the Lord, the veil is taken away. Now the Lord is the Spirit; and where the Spirit of the Lord is, there is liberty. But we all, with unveiled face, beholding as in a mirror the glory of the Lord, are being transformed into the same image from glory to glory, just as by the Spirit of the Lord." 2 Corinthians 3:15-18

Therefore, the unique blessing of year 2021 is the widespread emphasis of the Holy Spirit throughout the body of Christ worldwide to

- More abundantly expose the emptiness of licentious concept of righteousness,

- Further discourage the legalistic concept of righteousness while;

- Drawing all into the scripturally balanced understanding of the true concept of righteousness as the state of the heart received by faith in Christ to love God so wholeheartedly as to steadfastly cultivate such intimate fellowship with the Holy Spirit in the word of God, prayers and heartfelt desires to win souls and to give God pleasure in all things.

"3 Blessed are the poor in spirit,
For theirs is the kingdom of heaven.
4 Blessed are those who mourn,
For they shall be comforted.
5 Blessed are the meek,
For they shall inherit the earth.
6 Blessed are those who hunger and thirst for righteousness,
For they shall be filled.
16 Let your light so shine before men, that they may see your good works and glorify your Father in heaven."
Matthew 5:3-6; 16

"Therefore do not worry, saying, 'What shall we eat?' or 'What shall we drink?' or 'What shall we wear?' For after all these things the Gentiles seek. For your heavenly Father knows that you need all these things. But seek first the kingdom of God and His righteousness, and all these things shall be added to you."
Matthew 6:31-33

God Wants To Positively Transform Your Experience

Therefore, the Holy Spirit is calling our attention to the true righteousness in Christ in the year 2021 in order to transform our concept and experience of righteousness from narrow minded legalism and sense of condemnation which demotivates big dreams and great achievements to the experience of true righteousness initiated by the election of grace and operated by the Holy Spirit in the liberating sprinkling of the Blood of Jesus and empowerment of His Truth in the Bible.

Therefore, as from this year 2021

- You will stop the negative comparison that makes you look down on yourself;

- You will begin to cultivate the divine assurance that you will eventually become great because you have been elected (as Abraham was) by grace;

- You will begin to positively see your failures as part of your divine trainings and that the sufferings you have to endure are for your sanctification

- You will better understand that it is the sacrifices that you choose to make for Christ and His Kingdom that will determine the level of your spiritual growth and greatness in His Kingdom.

In the long run, for as long as you continue to abide in the love of Christ, you will surely win because God has accepted responsibility for that.

It Is Also About Your Eternal Glory

"For as by one man's disobedience many were made sinners, so also by one Man's obedience many will be made righteous. Moreover the law entered that the offense might abound. But where sin abounded, grace abounded much more, so that as sin reigned in death, even so grace might reign through righteousness to eternal life through Jesus Christ our Lord." Romans 5:19-21

The original plan of God is for you to reign with Christ as His joint-heir in eternity. True righteousness in Christ will enable you to begin to have a foretaste of that eternal glory here on earth. This is one way to further encourage your pursuit of abiding with Christ forever.

Operation Holiness and Righteousness

Sinĵe Tuesday, December 1, 2020 until Sunday, February 7, 2021, we continue to meet on Sundays at 9am, Tuesdays at 6pm and Fridays at 10pm for teaching, prayers and thanksgivings ministrations to facilitate the necessary spiritual surgical operations by the Holy Spirit to renew our minds and transform our hearts for the glorious experience of the life and blessings of true righteousness of Christ in our daily activities as true disciples of Christ.

Please endeavour to be part of these operations either physically or online

(www.mixlr.com/chrisfo;
facebook: www.facebook.com/christianfoundations1;
Twitter: @chrisfo12;
YouTube: Christian Foundations CHRISFO)

This will enable you to more effectively use the prayer points inspired by the Holy Spirit in this Prayer Bulletin.

2021 is the year of the righteousness of Christ in your life, health, career, ministry, marriage, home, children, finance, etc. In Jesus Name. Amen.

Your servant for Christ's sake,
Kehinde A. Osinowo
Pastor 0656211220

SCRIPTURES FOR THE YEAR

Psalm 112:1-10

1   Blessed is the man who
fears the Lord,
Who delights greatly in His
commandments.
2   His descendants will be
mighty on earth;
The generation of the
upright will be blessed.
3   Wealth and riches will
be in his house,
And his righteousness
endures forever.
4   Unto the upright there
arises light in the darkness;
He is gracious, and full of
compassion, and righteous.
5   A good man deals
graciously and lends;
He will guide his affairs
with discretion.
6   Surely he will never be
shaken;
The righteous will be in
everlasting remembrance.
7   He will not be afraid of
evil tidings;
His heart is steadfast,
trusting in the Lord.
8   His heart is
established;
He will not be afraid,
Until he sees his desire
upon his enemies.
9   He has dispersed
abroad,
He has given to the poor;
His righteousness endures
forever;

His horn will be exalted
with honor.
10 The wicked will see it
and be grieved;
He will gnash his teeth and
melt away;
The desire of the wicked
shall perish.

Isaiah 54:11-17

11 "O you afflicted one,
Tossed with tempest, and
not comforted,
Behold, I will lay your
stones with colorful gems,
And lay your foundations
with sapphires.
12 I will make your
pinnacles of rubies,
Your gates of crystal,
And all your walls of
precious stones.
13 All your children shall
be taught by the Lord,
And great shall be the
peace of your children.
14 In righteousness you
shall be established;
You shall be far from
oppression, for you shall
not fear;
And from terror, for it shall
not come near you.
15 Indeed they shall surely
assemble, but not because
of Me.
Whoever assembles
against you shall fall for
your sake.
16 "Behold, I have created
the blacksmith
Who blows the coals in the
fire,
Who brings forth an
instrument for his work;
And I have created the
spoiler to destroy.
17 No weapon formed
against you shall prosper,
And every tongue which
rises against you in
judgment

You shall condemn.
This is the heritage of the
servants of the Lord,
And their righteousness is
from Me,"
Says the Lord.

Romans 5:17-21

17   For if by the one man's offense death reigned through the one, much more those who receive abundance of grace and of the gift of righteousness will reign in life through the One, Jesus Christ.)
18   Therefore, as thrŁugh one man's offense judgment came to all men, resulting in condemnation, even so through one Man's righteous act the free gift came to all men, resulting in justification of life. 19 For as by one man's disobedience many were made sinners, so also by one Man's obedience many will be made righteous. 20 Moreover the law entered that the offense might abound. But where sin abounded, grace abounded much more, 21 so that as sin reigned in death, even so grace might reign through righteousness to eternal life through Jesus Christ our Lord.

---

2 Corinthians 5:14-21

14 For the love of Christ compels us, because we judge thus: that if One died for all, then all died; 15 and He died for all, that those who live should live no longer for themselves, but for Him who died for them and rose again.

16   Therefore, from now on, we regard no one according to the flesh. Even though we have known Christ according to the flesh, yet now we know Him thus no longer.
17   Therefore, if anyone is in Christ, he is a new creation; old things have passed away; behold, all things have become new.
18 Now all things are of God, who has reconciled us to Himself through Jesus Christ, and has given us the ministry of reconciliation,
19 that is, that God was in Christ reconciling the world to Himself, not imputing their trespasses to them, and has committed to us the word of reconciliation.
20   Now then, we are ambassadors for Christ, as though God were pleading through us: we implore you on Christ's behalf, be reconciled to God. 21 For He made Him who knew no sin to be sin for us, that we might become the righteousness of God in Him.

Titus 3:3-7

3   For we ourselves were also once foolish, disobedient, deceived, serving various lusts and pleasures, living in malice and envy, hateful and hating one another. 4 But when the kindness and the love of God our Savior toward man appeared, 5 not by works of righteousness which we have done, but according to His mercy He saved us, through the washing of

regeneration and renewing
of the Holy Spirit, 6 whom
He poured out on us
abundantly through Jesus
Christ our Savior, 7 that
having been justified by His
grace we should become
heirs according to the hope
of eternal life.

I AM A TREE OF RIGHTEOUSNESS IN CHRIST

Faith Platform: *"...That they may be called trees of righteousness, the planting of the LORD, that He may be glorified."* Isaiah 61:3

Bible Text: Isaiah 61:1-10

Voice of Hope: 2021 is a significantly prophetic year for all of us – as individuals, church and as families and homes. To some it is a year of vengeance but to all who wholeheartedly revere God and seek to please Him in His Son Jesus Christ, it is a year of significantly positive transformation. It is a year when the Holy Spirit will help me to practically internalise the truth that on the day I first gave my life to Jesus, God accepted the responsibility to make me become like Christ. He imputed the righteousness of Christ in me and made His grace available to me by which I am to reign in life and eternity by the LORDSHIP of Jesus Christ. Therefore, the law of the Spirit of life in Christ

Jesus has set me free from the law of the sin and death with its operative traits of condemnation, shame, discouragement, inferiority complex, small-mindedness, sluggish performance, failures, etc. It is time for me to begin to receive big dreams and make great achievements in Christ. In Jesus Name. Amen.

PRAYER POINTS

DAY 1

1. Heavenly Father, I thank You for Your eternal love by which You sent Your only begotten Son Jesus Christ and You fully equipped Him to make me one of Your sons

2. Thank You, Father that in accordance with Your foreknowledge You elected me to become a joint heir with Christ.

3. Thank You for how Your Holy Spirit has continuously wooed me since in my mother's womb by His sanctification that brought me to obey the gospel.

4. Thank You that You have now put me under the continuous sprinkling of the Blood of Jesus

5. Thank You, Father that You have now securely planted me as a tree of Your righteousness; I am Your workmanship in Christ Jesus.

DAY 2

6. Heavenly Father, thank You for graciously bringing me into this new year of Your righteousness in Christ.

7.   Thank You that You have exempted me and my family, etc. from the scourge of COVID-19

8.   This year Your Spirit will always work in me to fear You in righteousness and serve You with true integrity of heart.

9É   Therefore, the Spirit of Jesus will keep me in His fellowship to guard, guide and help me by counselling and revealing secrets of life to me.

10.   This year, I will further cultivate my fellowship with Your Spirit by daily meditation in Your Word, praying for power to please You and being useful for You by following the instructions of our Church authority.

DAY 3

11.   The Holy Spirit will enhance my confidence before God and men this year

12.   I will receive increasingly deeper assurance that You have accepted me as Your son; I am reconciled with You in Christ Jesus; You are no more angry to punish me but You are committed to help me.

13.   This year I will live in further consciousness of Jesus as the Author and Finisher of my faith; I will no more let my natural weaknesses define me or determine my endeavours.

14.   I will live in the consciousness that my Father in heaven watches my back; He will justify and vindicate me and avenge me of my enemies.

15.   I will no more fear bad dreams; I will cancel their effects by faith.

DAY 4

16.   Thank You LORD for what Your Spirit is already doing to renew my mind by Your Word so that my heart and approach to life are being transformed to experience the peace, boldness, wisdom, diligence and prosperity of righteousness in this new year.

17.   This year, I will cultivate the voice of the Holy Spirit as He applies Your precious promises to my heart to give me hope of heaven.

18.   You will heal my brokenness and release me from under the captivity of the things mightier than me.

19.   You will bring me out of the prison of my background limitations, inherited demonic strongholds and natural inadequacies.

20.   This year, I will cultivate the righteousness of Christ and become increasingly positive and bold like a lion; the Lion of the Tribe of Judah operates through me.

DAY 5

21.   This is the year of righteousness of Christ in my life, health, career, ministry, marriage, home, children, finance, etc.

22.   I will be a salt of Christ in my relationships

23.   I will let the light of Christ shine through me, so that

many will glorify God because of me.

24. In the times of temptations and trials, I will cultivate the consolation of Scriptures and comfort of the Holy Spirit.

25. I will always give God my thanks, praise and worship.

DAY 6

26. God will use me to change the culture aLd spiritual status of my lineage.

27. Father, please give me an unrelenting burden for the salvation of the souls of every member of my extended family

28. LORD please provide adequately for me to be able to care for them physically, materially, financially, etc. in a way that will draw them to Your love.

29. Father, please prompt me always to fulfil my portion in the mission of CHRISFO to rebuild the foundations of persons, families, churches, communities, nations, etc. upon the grace and Truth of Jesus.

30. Holy Spirit, please help me to the etent that my lifestyle and works will make people call me (and members of my family, our church, etc.) true sons of God and priests of His righteousness.

DAY 7

31. O LORD, help me not to backslide but I and my household will continue to abound in the works of the gospel.

32. The Christian commission is global, please help me, my family and our church to make disciples of many more nations for Christ.

33. Anywhere we go, empower us to reconcile men and women to You and among themselves in Christ.

34. Help us to be divinely empowered peace makers at personal, family, household, church, communities and even national levels.

35. Help me to grow in Christlikeness so that I, my family and those we bring to Christ will enter into eternal life in Christ.

THE SALT AND LIGHT OF CHRIST OPERATES IN AND THROUGH ME

Faith Platform: *"that you may become blameless and harmless, children of God without fault in the midst of a crooked and perverse generation, among whom you shine as lights in the world"* Philippians 2:15

Bible Text: Matthew 5:1-16

Voice of Hope: Thank You LORD for helping me to internalise the truth that I am Your righteousness in Christ. (2 Cor. 5:21). Not because I have become perfect but because I am Your own "work in progress" in Christ Jesus and You have accepted the responsibility to make me become like Christ for as long as I also sincerely desire to be so. Therefore, this year, You will help me to further grow in the nature of Christ in my character and interpersonal relationships and to always take the trouble to let others know that it is Christ that is working in me so that they also may become sincere disciples of Christ. (1 Peter 3:15, 16)

DAY 8

36. Thank You Father that You have made me Your righteousness in Christ.

37. Now there is no condemnation for me because I am Your workmanship in Christ Jesus. I am truly grateful.

38. Thank You that You now respond to my sins and failures with sympathy and necessary divine strategies to help me out of the underlying weaknesses. I am completely accepted in Christ (Heb. 4:15)

39. Help me LORD not to take Your redemptive kindness for granted; deliver me from every form of self-indulgence that the devil wants to use to make me cut off myself from your redemption.

40. This year, I will grow in my love for God and my pursuit of Christlikeness in all I say and do.

DAY 9

41. Holy Spirit please help me to continue to be poor in the Spirit that I may eventually inherit the kingdom of God.

42. Please help me to continue to cultivate a broken heart so that I can easily be convicted of my sins. I will not be among those who would not know their own sins until the day of Judgement (1 Tim. 5:24)

43. Help me to quickly confess my sins with sorrows of genuine repentance that I may always be

strengthened by the comfort of the Holy Spirit.

44.	Holy Ghost empower me to be meek that I may inherit the earth.

45.	Help me to relate and talk to others (irrespective of their age or socio-economic status) in a way to enhance their sense of value and hope. Then You will attract favour to me.

DAY 10

46.	Help me LORD to always hunger and thirst for Your righteousness by giving myself to the discipline of Bible meditation and prayers.

47.	Help me to tremble at Your Word and prayerfully seek for Your strength until I put Your word in practice.

48.	Holy Spirit, please help me to keep my conscience alive by fellowship with the Holy Spirit and the spiritual experience I gain by serving You in our Church.

49.	Heavenly Father, please help me to abide in Your mercy that I may always experience Your ready forgiveness.

50.	In the same manner empower me to be understanding and merciful to those who offend and hurt me so I can readily forgive them.

DAY 11

51.	This year, I receive more grace to be single-minded in my pursuit of Christ.

52. Help me that even in my thoughts, imaginations, words and actions, I will always want to know and do only what pleases God according to the Doctrine of Christ in the Bible.

53. Help me LORD, always to sanctify You in my heart, to worship You in Spirit and Truth that I may more easily discern Your will

54. Deliver me from the attraction, distraction and defilement of the world that makes me unknowingly rebel against Your written commandment and inspired guidance.

55. In everything, help me to pursue Jesus as the Author and Finisher of my faith; to always want to act and/or react only as Jesus would do according to the Bible.

DAY 12

56. I want others to recognise me as Your son by my words and actions, please make me a peace maker, from my heart.

57. As far as it depends on me, help me to live peaceably with all others (Rom. 12:18)

58. Grant me the meekness to answer harsh and unfair words with soft and reconciliatory words.

59. Help me never to ignore those who feel offended by me but to seek reconciliation with them (Matt. 5:23, 24)

60. Where necessary, help me to get third party intervention that I may reconcile with those who

offend me or feel offended by me (Matt. 18:15-17)

DAY 13

61. Father, I want to inherit the kingdom of heaven as well as to be prosperously successful here on earth, please give me a mind-set ready to suffer for being Your righteousness in Christ.

62. Grant me the spiritual and moral fortitude to bear the opposition, attacks and afflictions that might be hauled at me because I stand on the truth that Jesus is the only means of salvation of God (John 14:6)

63. Grant me the meekness to be content with whatever positon I am given in the Church and not to practise bitter envying against others that might appear to have been favoured at my expense.

64. I resist you satan, you will not use my ego to cause disharmony in our church, I will be submissive to the church authority and be accommodating with the brethren.

65. Help me to be strengthened by the understanding that You will reward me bountifully here on earth and more in heaven for every form of unfair dishonour I endure from outside the church because of my faithfulness to Christ and His Word.

DAY 14

66. Help me to understand that it is only the dishonour which I endure and the insults I bear for Christ that

You will recognise and reward (1 Pet. 4:13-15)

67. Help me to understand that the only way my sufferings can be linked with Christ is if I preach the gospel.

68. Without my preaching the gospel, I may be rewarded on earth for suffering for righteousness but I will not be rewarded in heaven for suffering for Christ and His gospel. LORD, please delver me from such foolishness and loss.

69. Help me to make it a point of duty to preach the gospel everywhere I go so my life-style can be identified with Christ and bring glory to God.

70. Help me to see every human relationship as an opportunity to preach the gospel and not waste it.

OUR CHURCH IS ESTABLISHED IN THE RIGHTEOUSNESS OF CHRIST

Faith Platform: *"...See, I have set before you an open door, and no one can shut it; for you have a little strength, have kept My word, and have not denied My name."* Revelation 3:8

Bible Text: Revelation 3:7-13

Voice of Hope: Thank You LORD that in this year when you are further encouraging the confidence of Your children as Your righteousness in Christ, the devil will not be able to manipulate the spiritual, social and moral environment of our Church against that Your purpose. As a Ministry and Mission, You have called on us to enter into the fulfilment of the Philadelphia Church (Rev. 3:7-13) on a global basis. This year You will work in our Church Leadership to be more sensitive and obedient to the Holy Spirit in order to further enhance the spiritual capacities of our congregations and members to experience the reality of our election as the righteousness of God in Christ.

PRAYER POINTS

DAY 15

71. LORD Jesus, we worship You as You more fully reveal Yourself among us in this Church as holy, true, having the key of David and that what You open, no one shuts and what You shut, no one opens.

72. We thank You for Your testimony about our Church Leadership. Help our Pastor and those working with him not to backslide, falter or fall

73. Thank You LORD that although our strength is little but You have continued to enable us to do the works that are acceptable to You. Please deliver our pastor and leaders from personal weaknesses and demonic strategies to defile us.

74. Thank You LORD that although our strength is little, You have and will continue to empower us to keep Your Word

75. You have and will continue to enable us not to deny Your Name.

DAY 16

76. Father we thank You for our Pastor and all those working directly with him.

77. You have delivered us, help them not to unwittingly return our church environment to a place of legalism and hypocrisy.

78. LORD, please continue to uphold our pastor and his team from the snares of Nicolaitans, Balaam, Jezebel,

etc. and their noisome pestilence. Our Church environment will not become either compromising, corrupt or spiritually dead.

79. We cast out the spirits of Pergamos, Thyatira, Sardis and Laodicea from our Pastor and his team.

80. Our pastor will not become worldly permissive, sexually immoral, hypocritical and/or materialistic either in secret, private, open or public.

DAY 17

81. Our Pastor will continue to keep Your Word; our Church environment will continue to be conducive for the efficacy of Your word.

82. Our Pastor will continue to uphold Your name and our Church environment will continue to be conducive for the operation of the Holy Spirit.

83. Ĥur members will be increasingly traĿsformed by the renewal of their minds in the Word of God.

84. The Holy Spirit will increasingly perform miracles, signs and wonders to change the lives of our members for better and to attract others to Christ.

85. Our members will prosper and be wealthy but always love and obey Christ in His Word more that money; we will not backslide to become a mammonic church.

DAY 18

86. Thank You LORD that You know our weaknesses that our enemies want to exploit and You are set to help us

unto victory.

87. O LORD, please expose those among us who are around us as friends but have been sent by the devil to spy, weaken and defile us. Bring them to genuine repentance or expel the rebellious from among us.

88. We release the fire of the Holy Ghost upon everyone and anything that has been sent to us from the synagogue of satan. Let the unrepentant be expelled and redeemed converted.

89. O LORD, please expose and destroy any lie of satan that might be spreading underground among us as brotherly fellowship, friendship, counsel or unarticulated influence. Bring their human drivers into the light and repentance of the gospel

90. Satan, the LORD will always bruise your head under our feet.

DAY 19

91. Thank You LORD that You will continue to use our Church to convict all sorts of sinners and save the souls of church goers, hypocrites, muslims, pagans, idol-worshippers, occultists, sexually immoral, extortionists, etc.

92. Holy Spirit You will help us to always glorify and lift Jesus higher than any other force, principle or personality.

93. Holy Spirit You will help us to always operate only by your leadings in our personal and church meetings

and fellowships.

94. You will always quickly expose human and demonic representatives of the devil and make them worship the LORD Jesus at our feet.

95. Thank You LORD that You have loved us and You will continue to prove it to outsiders. Help us to also love You more and more.

DAY 20

96. Father, we thank You for the door of the gospel You have opened for us.

97. Thank You that no third party power can either shut or diminish the opportunities, help and resources available for us in that door.

98. LORD, please help us not to waste the door by unbelief, fear, laziness or pride, etc.

99. We cast out the spirit of "divide and rule" from among us or between us and our gospel collaborators.

100. By Your grace, O LORD, we will enter fully into the door You have opened for Solemn Assembly Tours, Church Planting, Bible School, ACCF, etc.

DAY 21

101. Our church will continue to be prayerful, seek to be guided by the Bible and be sensitive to the Holy Spirit.

102. LORD, You have renewed the ears of our spirits, we will always hear and obey what Your Holy Spirit is saying to our Church.

103. As a church, individuals and homes, we will live our lives in the consciousness that Jesus will soon come back to take us home.

104. We will not be ensnared by the love of this world, we will overcome and be raptured with Jesus when He comes again.

105. You will help us to persevere to the end; we will not be overwhelmed by whatever trials You allow upon this world.

I WILL EXPERIENCE THE PROSPERITY OF THE RIGHTEOUS IN MY HEALTH, CAREER, TRADE, FINANCE, ETC.

Faith Platform: *"Beloved, I pray that you may prosper in all things and be in health, just as your soul prospers."* 3 John 1:2

Bible Text: Psalm 1:1-6; Proverbs 3:1-10; 2 Corinthians 9:6-11

Voice of Hope: Biblical righteousness is the state of the heart that reveres God so much as not to want to displease Him but to increasingly love Him and give Him pleasure and glory; after all, that is why He made the human race. This year, I will become more committed to see God in all that relates to my health, career, trade, finance, etc. and to seek for, discover, and fulfil His good pleasure. Therefore, my health, career, trade, finance, etc. will more effectively bring glory to God and draw more people to put their trust in Jesus.

2021 CELEBRATION CAMP

Wed. Sept. 1st - Sun. Sept. 5th

Chapel of Beauty & Glory
SALVATION HOUSE ESTATE,
Baale Akinosi, Ajuwon - Akute

Join us LIVE ON

- mixlr.com/chrisfo
- Christian Foundations CHRISFO
- ChristianFoundations
- Christian Foundations-CHRISFO

CHRISTIAN FOUNDATIONS MISSIONARY CHURCH (CFMC)

PRAYER POINTS

DAY 22

106. This year, I will stop following any counsel that is contrary to the Truth of Jesus in The Bible.

107. Therefore, I will give myself to become conversant with the Truth of Jesus in the Bible so I can discern and avoid the counsel of the ungodly.

108. I will no more allow myself to be influenced by the flashy lifestyle and pleasures of sinners.

109. Therefore, LORD help me to spend quality time in prayers at least three (morning, afternoon, night) times a day for the inner strength to flee from the allurements of sinners.

110. O LORD, irrespective of how busy I am in my career, help me to be committed to some spiritual responsibilities in the church that will preoccupy my mind and prevent me from sitting and chatting with scorners.

DAY 23

111. This year, I will further cultivate abiding in the Word of Christ that I may be His disciple indeed; I will know His Truth and He will set my heart and life free to seek and please Him.

112. In every situation – trial, temptation or godly opportunity, I will cultivate the discipline of responding by praying effectively in tongues and by

the relevant Word of God.

113. By prayer and obedience to the word of God, my life will become a stream of God orchestrated miracles.

114. I will prosper in my health, career, trade, finance, etc. as and when due.

115. As I seek and follow the guidance of the Holy Spirit, whatever I do will prosper.

DAY 24

116. By consistent quiet time of prayers and meditation in the Bible, I dwell in the secret place of the Most High.

117. With a mind-set and sincere efforts to remember and obey the word throughout the day, I abide under the shadow of the Almighty.

118. Those that set them against me will be blown away with their weapons by the wind.

119. Those who speak evil and/or orchestrate slanders against me shall fall in judgement.

120. The LORD shall guide and protect me and raise me above the wicked plans of the enemy.

DAY 25

121. Father, in accordance with Your will, I will prosper in my spirit, soul, body and in the works of my hands.

122. Jesus became poor that I might become rich (2 Cor. 8:9). Therefore, this year, I will follow divine guidance into my prosperity and financial wealth.

123. This year, I will not lean in my own understanding but I will trust the LORD with all my heart so that I will not lack any good thing due to me.

124. This year, I will further cultivate the fear of the LORD and an upright heart. Therefore the Angel of the LORD will always camp around me and my home to deliver me.

125. This year I will seek the face of the LORD and receive big dreams in my profession, trade and financial endeavours.

DAY 26

126. In my business relationships and transactions, I will not be wise in my own conceit; I will not let fear or pride force me to adopt ungodly ways.

127. I will fear the LORD and depart from evil practices

128. By this, the LORD will grant me inner peace, healthy body and strong bones.

129. I will make the LORD the centre of my work time-table and priority in the distribution of my profits. I will honour the LORD with my first fruits.

130. Therefore, the LORD will grant me favour to attract customers that will quickly pay me with high profit Ljargins.

DAY 27

131. Father grant me that I will be increasingly filled with the knowledge of Your will in all wisdom and spiritual

understanding.

132. That I will more perfectly walk worthy of You, fully pleasing You, being fruitful in every good work and increasing in Your knowledge.

133. So that I will always be strengthened with all might, according to Your glorious power for all patience and longsuffering with joy.

134. In this context, please grant me a full understanding of Your plans and the purpose I should pursue this new year in my health, career, trade, finance, etc.

135. This year, I will not beat about the bush.

DAY 28

136. Father, please help me to come up with the specific projects I should pursue this year in my career, business, trade, finance, etc.

137. Help me to maximise my present occupation to generate the time, talents, diligence and money to sow for the achievement of my goals this year.

138. Grant that behind every effort I put forward will always be how I will better support the ministry of our church to win souls and make disciples unto Christ.

139. Grant me the wisdom to distinguish between the seed You have given me to sow (in my business and the ministry of our church) and the seed that You have given me for bread. I will not eat the seed to be sown with the one for bread. I will be disciplined and self-

controlled

140. Thank You LORD, that You will multiply my seed sown and increase the fruits of my righteousness so that I will be enriched in everything for liberality to the gospel.

I WILL BUILD MY RELATIONSHIPS AND MARRIAGE ON THE RIGHTEOUSNESS OF CHRIST

Faith Platform: *"Be kindly affectionate to one another with brotherly love, in honor giving preference to one another"* Romans 12:10

Bible Text: Ephesians 5:1-33

Voice of Hope: This is the year of the righteousness of God in Christ. This year I will let my reverence to God determine how I respond to all and how and who I relate to closely. The LORD will deliver me from the snares of the fowler and their noisome pestilence and use me to draw many others to Christ.

PRAYER POINTS

DAY 29

141. As Joseph was kind towards his co-prisoners and one of them later recommended him to Pharaoh, so I will meekly relate with the fear of God and love to all I

come across.

142. This year, I receive deeper grace to operate in the divine nature of God in all my relationships

143. Help me, LORD, to walk in love so that I can bear necessary inconveniences to make the gospel attractive to others.

144. Father, please deliver me from my natural inclinations of wanting to enjoy either the body, intellect or other resources of others instead of thinking of how to facilitate the salvation of their souls.

145. O God, please help me to make my motive in my relationship with others righteous and a sacrifice of a sweet aroma to You in Christ.

DAY 30

146. Father, I desire that Your gift of righteousness to me in Christ will lead me to true holiness.

147. Father, please convict me and help me to truly repent of my pleasure in thinking, reading, watching and talking about all forms of ungodliness and covetousness.

148. Father, please grant me the inner strength and the grace to always flee from temptations to sexual immorality on social media and physical social meetings, including Christian fellowships.

149. Create in me a new heart and renew Your right Spirit within me so that I will not gratify my (sometimes

very strong) desires for sexual immorality.

150. I cast out the demons of sexual immorality. Satan you will not use my libido to take me to hell.

DAY 31

151. This year, I will not take God for granted; I will not turn the gift of righteousness into licentiousness.

152. O LORD, since even the righteous might be scarcely saved (1 Pet. 4:18), help me to always take heed lest I fall.

153. Help me to rise above careless practices of my Christian faith

154. Deliver me from filthiness, foolish talking, coarse jesting, etc.

155. Help me to fill my heart with Your Word and thanksgiving, that I may be holy.

DAY 32

156. I pull down the stronghold of mammon in my thoughts, words and actions; I break the ensnaring power of the love of money.

157. Satan, you will not use the love of money to take me to hell. I will increasingly love God with all my heart, soul and might. Satan you cannot have any hold on me.

158. Covetousness is idol-worshipping; I receive grace not to desire any man, woman, girl, boy, gold, silver, power or connection contrary to the will of God. My

relationship with other people or things will be controlled by my love for God.

159. Jesus has allotted an inheritance for me in heaven, I will not backslide to hell; I will not lose my inheritance.

160. I will not be deceived and will watch unto eternal life and glory.

DAY 33

161. Holy Spirit, please help me to live in the consciousness that I am in a spiritual battle.

162. I worship You Father that although the powers of darkness from under which I was redeemed still want to get me back but they have no power to touch me for as long as I abide in Christ.

163. Therefore, help me to be guided only by the Truth of Jesus in the Bible and not by tradition, culture or family ties.

164. Help me no more to keep any covenant of secrecy with the devil. I will quickly confess my sins and expose any demonic inspired secrets.

165. I refuse to have any fellowship with unfruitful works of darkness but rather I will always prayerfully expose them

DAY 34

166. O LORD, please help me to begin to walk circumspectly and not as fools

167. Help me to be motivated by the love of God and my

faith in Jesus and NOT fear, pride or lusts in my relationships

168. Help me to become more deliberate in choosing my close acquaintants.

169. Holy Spirit, lead me to spend time with those who will edify me in Christ and direct me away from those who will stealthy tempt me and ensnare me with sins

170. Deliver me from the attraction of lusts; do not let me be ensnared into marriage by either the pride of life or lust of the flesh and eyes.

DAY 35

171. I will marry in the LORD. Help me to ensure that my future spouse is a true child of God.

172. Help me to investigate and be sure his/her outlook to life is Christian and scriptural and in agreement with mine.

173. Help me to ensure that he/she already has a ministry in his/her church that is complimentary to mine and that he/she already has a spiritual ambition that is attuned with mine.

174. O LORD, in Your mercy, do not allow me to marry a spouse that would be a burden on my Christian faith and a hindrance to my spiritual ambition.

175. Grant me the spiritual maturity to patiently, diligently and prayerfully wait on You until I am sure of Your will before I go into any relationship with a view to marriage; even in business.

MY HOME, CHILDREN, ETC. BEAR THE FRUITS OF RIGHTEOUSNESS IN CHRIST

Faith Platform: *"For I have known him, in order that he may command his children and his household after him, that they keep the way of the LORD, to do righteousness and justice, that the LORD may bring to Abraham what He has spoken to him."* Genesis 18:19

Bible Text: Gen. 18:17-19; Deut. 6:4-9; Psalm 127; Eph. 6:1-4

Voice of Hope: It is very significant to note that the school that God set up to equip human beings for their basic roles in life is the home. That is why, it has been severally observed by pundits throughout history that in spite of the technical, professional, intellectual and/or management training available in prestigious institutions of learning and the laurels acquired by many diligent students, success in life has been more fundamentally influenced by the home upbringing of the champions. Of course, the home front has since suffered much satanic attacks and distractions and has become increasingly deteriorating.

So God in His immense love sent His only begotten Son, Jesus, for the redemption of mankind and rebuilding of the home spiritual structure. The LORD Jesus, having accomplished that assignment has given the Church the responsibility to bring all families into redemption and rebuilding of the spiritual structure of their homes in the righteousness of Christ.

By the grace of God, this year, I and my home, family, children, marriage, etc. will more fully align with this divine benevolence.

PRAYER POINTS
DAY 36

176. Heavenly Father, thank You that Your plan for the redemption of the human race is not only about independent individuals but also about whole homes.
177. Thank You Father because Your Word promises that if I believe in the LORD Jesus Christ, I will be saved and my household with me (Acts 16:31)
178. Father, it is only in Your Word that I find consolation and hope for my marriage, home, children, etc. Thank You that You are faithful to Your Word.
179. Help me to search Your Word and pray for practical wisdom of how to bring my home into the experience

of Your promises

180. Please always empower me to obey the wisdom that You give me from Your Word.

DAY 37

181. Father, I worship You that Your Word is not a lie. There are examples in the Bible (like Abraham, Jacob, even David) and in contemporary church history (like Jonathan Edwards) in whose homes Your Word has been fulfilled.

182. Father, You chose me the way You chose Abraham, please help me to order my household into Your righteousness and prosperity like his.

183. O LORD, I have many spiritual and moral challenges in my life, marriage, home and children. Abraham also had but You gave him victory. Please help me also to overcome.

184. Father, You have called me and my home for assignment on earth and glory in eternity. Help me to internalise this call and help every member of my household to also internalise Your call

185. By Your grace, my home and I will fulfil Your purpose on earth and have an abundant entrance into Your eternal kingdom.

DAY 38

186. Abraham and his lineage inherited Your promise because he constrained his household to obey You but

Lot, Eli and Saul failed because they were indulgent with their households.

187. Help me to love and care for my family but never to indulge them contrary to Your Word.

188. Saul and his lineage were rejected because Saul himself was not faithful to Your Word; please grant me the grace to always revere and obey You like Abraham and to be Your approved example to my household.

189. The lineage of Lot became an enduring abomination before God because Lot did not put his wife under the control of Your Word. Help me to love and sacrifice for my wife but never to let her manipulate me and my children away from Your righteousness.

190. Eli and his lineage were cut off from the eternal glory of priesthood because Eli did not constrain his children to honour You. Please always give me the inner strength to compel my children and household to honour You in all things.

DAY 39

191. Help me LORD to continue to grow as a true disciple of Christ indeed and bear the fruits of the righteousness of Christ in my conduct as a Christian man (woman), husband (wife), father (mother) and minister of the gospel.

192. Grant me the discipline to always present every member of my household before You in prayers and to know Your thoughts and what You want me to do

about them.

193. Help me to create time to bond with members of my household together and as unique individuals. Grant me the discipline, sacrifice, meekness and courage to do this successfully.

194. Help me to formally teach Your Word to my household in Family Devotions and disciplined participation in the Church.

195. But give me the wisdom and dexterity to apply Your Word both in the informal social settings and during handling of serious challenges and joys of life.

DAY 40

196. Teach and help me to model total trust in God in every situation and for every need of life.

197. Help me to create the home atmosphere that makes trust in God and obedience to His Word indispensable.

198. Please grant my wife (me as the mother of the house) the spiritual ambition to be wise and virtuous so that she (I) will help me (my husband) to build our home and not scatter us.

199. Grant me the wisdom to accept that I am only Your steward over my children and our household. You are the real Father of my children and the true owner of my household.

200. Help me (and my wife) to lead our children to develop a personal faith in Jesus as their personal LORD and

Saviour and a heartfelt assurance that God is their personal Father.

DAY 41

201. LORD please grant me a forgiving spirit towards my children when they offend and hurt me.
202. Ẽonstrain my wife to help our children to appreciate my fatherly love and sacrifices for them and the household.
203. Whatever be the case draw my heart towards my children and their hearts towards me in Christ that no curse or demonic activity can ever prevail in my home (Malachi 4:6)
2Ě4. Grant that my children be taught of You that they may have the wisdom to play the roles You have assigned for them in my home.
205. My children shall not waste my legacies but shall build on it and expand it to maximise their destinies in Christ.

DAY 42

206. My children shall not be children of Belial but shall obey me to follow the narrow path that leads to eternal life in Christ.
207. My children shall not fall into false doctrines; they shall faithfully abide in the love, grace and truth of the LORD Jesus in the Bible
208. My children shall fear God, be kindhearted and obey

God to honour and care for me and their mother in our old age

209. God will give each of my children spouses that will become my own children and significantly contribute to the expansion of our family legacies in Christ.

210. I will see my children's children and the prosperity of the Body of Christ in the land of the living.

MY FRUITS IN CHRIST WILL ABIDE TO ETERNAL GLORY

Faith Platform: *"You did not choose Me, but I chose you and appointed you that you should go and bear fruit, and that your fruit should remain, that whatever you ask the Father in My name He may give you."* John 15:16

Bible Text: John 15:1-16

Voice of Hope: Thank You LORD because I am not rejected, I have been chosen as a branch of Christ to bear fruits through my life, marriage, ministry, home, career, etc. I have been elected by God the Father in the sanctification of the Spirit unto obedience. This year and beyond I will continue to grow in a mind-set of a broken heart and contrite spirit, as I seek to obey God in every aspect of my life and endeavours. I will continually bear fruits of repentance, righteousness and soul-winning that will abide and abound to eternal glory in Christ.

PRAYER POINTS

DAY 43

211. O LORD Jesus I worship You because You are the True Vine, the Father is the Vinedresser. You are righteous and holy. All things exist in and through You.

212. Thank You because I am Your branch. You have chosen me to be an extension of all that You are and do.

213. I will be a model of Your beauty, holiness and righteousness in my marriage, home, work, neighbourhood, extended family, church, etc. I will bear fruits.

214. I repent of my barrenness and lack of productivity in my Christian life. I am sorry in every way I wasted grace. Show me mercy O LORD.

215. I repent of my bitterness, my unwillingness to pursue peace with members of my family, parent, children, spouse, boss, employee, brother/sister, etc.

DAY 44

216. Thank You LORD for the grace that I have received from You to bear fruits. You will help me to give myself more to You so that I can bear more fruits that will abound to eternity.

217. Thank You for Your word that You have sent to me. You will help me to receive Your Word by spending time in personal Bible Study, family devotion, fellowship meetings, etc.

218. I will be committed to build my marriage, family and home on the Truth of Jesus in the Bible. I will give importance to family devotion.

219. My children will grow in grace and the knowledge of Jesus, they will not depart from it. They will be taught by the LORD to make life decisions based on God's word. They will not give up their faith even at the face of dire circumstances and challenges.

220. My home and children will not be among the nations that will be turned to hell. My fruits will abide to eternal glory.

DAY 45

221. LORD, I acknowledge that I can do nothing without You. Help me to live my daily life in consciousness of this truth.

222. This truth will motivate me to seek you in prayers, fellowshipping with the Holy Spirit and study of Your Word.

223. I will cultivate a broken heart and contrite spirit. I will quickly acknowledge my sins and mistakes as I open my heart to Your Word.

224. I will always put Your Word ahead of my selfish desires, self-conceit, pride, etc. I will bear fruits worthy of emulation in my marriage, home, at work, in church and my community.

225. I will not settle for barren religion and legalism. I will

grow in love and passion for Christ, and in sacrificial love for the brethren and sinners.

DAY 46

226. Thank You that every curse working through my barrenness, unbelief, laziness, etc. has been broken in my life, marriage, home and in our Church. You will help me to continually live a life of repentance.
227. I break every curse working in my life as a result of the sluggishness of my heart to win souls and establish people in Christ.
228. Every demon working in my life, home, marriage because of my unwillingness to bear fruits and lack of spiritual ambition, be cast out now.
229. I will not be like a branch that bears thorns and briers. I will not be rejected. I have been elected and I will make my calling and election sure.
230. I will not be burned. I will not end up my life in hell. My marriage, home, children, family will not end up in hell. I will bear fruits to eternal glory. In Jesus Name.

DAY 47

231. Thank You for Your love for me. You gave Your life for me so that I will not go to hell but that I may have eternal life. I will abide in Your love.
232. I will show the same love to the people around me, my spouse, children, co-worker, neighbour, employer, employee, etc. I will make effort by the Holy Spirit to

win their souls to Christ.

233. Help me to understand that my love for my family, children is not just to provide for their material, physical needs but to ensure that their souls are saved, that they may not go to hell.

234. I will show sacrificial love to my family, children, parents, neighbour, co-worker even when they seem difficult and unreasonable, with the hope to win them to Christ.

235. I repent of my ego, pride, self-conceit. This year and beyond I will be motivated by the love of Christ in my relationship with people everywhere I go.

DAY 48

236. I will be given to soul-winning efforts in our local church. I will give house, car, money, children, energy, etc. to strengthen my Church's effort to win souls. I will have eternal rewards.

237. The joy of the LORD is my strength, I will not live a sickly and moody life. The countenance of Jesus is always shining on my face. My countenance will attract people and draw them to Jesus.

238. I will pursue peace with all men – members of our church, family, neigbours, etc. I will not by my ego, pride, bitterness, anger, etc. send people away from the church and Christ. I will not send people to hell.

239. I will be patient with and kind to people, even when they are unreasonable. I will stop responding to

unreasonable people as they deserve. I will always resMond to them in love.

240. I will be gentle and meek. I will not be indulgent, but tolerate other's weaknesses. I will be humble, relate with people of low estate and socio-economic class. I will bear fruits that will abide among all people.

DAY 49

241. LORD Jesus, I will keep it in mind that You are the One who chose me; I didn't choose You.

242. So, in all that I think, say or do, You will always be the Author and Finisher.

243. You chose me to be put in a place You had predetermined; deliver me from my carnal tendency to do and go to places I enjoy, irrespective of Your will.

244. You have chosen to make me a friend, I will neither become disrespectfully familiar with Your Word nor despiteful of Your servants.

245. I will not end up like the unprofitable servant. I will be submissive to our Church Authority, handle assignments diligently, draw many new members in and become profitable to Your Kingdom.

PRAYER FOR THE BODY OF CHRIST

Faith Platform: *"And I also say to you that you are Peter, and on this rock I will build My church, and the gates of Hades shall not prevail against it"* Matt. 16:18

Bible Text: Matt. 16:16-18; 28:18-20; Heb. 11:33, 34

Voice of Hope: The Church of Jesus Christ is the Body of Christ set up by the Father to continue and complete the work of the redemption of the human race that the Father committed to His Son when the Son was sent into the world in the human flesh. The Church is made up of men and women in whose hearts the Holy Spirit is at work to fulfil the redemption plans of the Father in accordance with the Truth of Jesus. The Church is the Godhead at work. Therefore, it cannot be defeated; it cannot be curtailed. It is the stone cut without hand in Dan. 2:34: the Church must prevail over the powers of Satan and his worldly structures.

PRAYER POINTS

1. Heavenly Father, we worship You as the Creator and Owner of all the human race.

2. We praise You, Father that You rule over the affairs of the human race and put their governments in the hands of those You have chosen.

3. You are the eventual Governor over all the earth and only Your own will is the unchangeable law.

4. Thank You, Father that You have set to use all these Your power and authority for the salvation of men and all Your creation.

5. Thank You our good God that You love all the world so much that You do not want any human to perish.

6. Thank You for sending Your Son Jesus Christ to the world in human likeness to save all human race.

7. Thank You that You have set up the Church for Him by which He would continue and finish the task.

8. Heavenly Father, we acknowledge that the foundation of the Church You set up is a personal conviction of members that Jesus is Your only begotten Son who has been with You from the beginning.

9. Thank You Father for the various visible gatherings of such people all over the world that make up Your Church – the Body of Your Son Jesus Christ.

10. Thank You LORD that the gates of hell will never prevail against this Body of Christ and its various church gatherings in their respective communities

all over the world.

11. Thank You LORD that all true Churches of Christ are invincible because the Spirit of Jesus is always at work among them.

12. Therefore, every power or force that comes against Your Church will be broken into pieces and anyone that Your Church comes against will be grounded into powder.

13. Holy Spirit please renew this understanding and conviction in all the various gatherings of the true Body of Christ in our nation and all over the world.

14. Father, give your Church divine courage to counteract the intimidating fear of the destructive and murderous activities of the anti-christs

15. We cast out the demons of fear and allurement from the Body of Christ.

16. Holy Spirit, please wake up Your Church into passionate soul-winning evangelism even if it has to appear like a suicide mission among violent anti-christs.

17. LORD please pour Your passion for soul-winning into Your Church and raise up men and women that will place their lives on the line for the salvation of all unreached including the violent anti-christs.

18. Heavenly Father, encourage passion for soul winning by stretching out Your hands to heal and that signs and wonders may be done through the name of Your holy Servant, Jesus.

19. Use Your Church to subdue kingdoms that are not conducive for the spread of the gospel – whether spiritual, traditional, social, political or economic.

20. Use Your Church to call peoples to the attention of the redemption in Christ by christian good works.

21. Use Your Church to fulfill Your promise of love and redemption.

22. Use Your Church to shut the mouths of demonic powers and their rulers that seek to resist Your Church.

23. We quench the violence of spiritual, demonic, moral or physical fire set against Your Church and communities ordained for redemption.

24. Holy Spirit, help us in Your Church to always escape the swords of ethno-religious fanatics.

25. Holy Spirit help us to allow You to turn our weakness into Your miraculous strength.

26. Make us bold and courageous to resist the violence of the anti-christs and turn them to flee.

27. Do not let those who are meant for salvation in our communities be scared or killed before they come to Christ.

28. Raise up political governments and social influence that will oppose and break the backbone of ethno-religious terrorists groups.

29. Put people in the UN leadership and the influential governments of the world that will create socio-political environments conducive for the spread of the

gospel.

30. We thank You for increased salvation among Jews and
    Gentiles.

PRAYER FOR OUR NATION

Faith Platform: *'And he who overcomes, and keeps My works until the end, to him I will give power over the nations'* Rev. 2:26

Bible Text: Psalm 2: 1-12; Acts 17;26,27

Voice of Hope: The Church of Jesus Christ is not powerless. When we are focused on what GOD wants us to do then we rule our nation on our knees like Elijah in Israel and Daniel in Babylon

PRAYER POINTS

1. Heavenly Father we worship You as the Most High and the only One who is in charge of all things
2. Thank You for Your love that gives us ordinary mortals, access to Your presence in Christ
3. Thank You for Your mercy that gives us room for repentance and forgiveness
4. Thank You for Your grace that always give us

another chance and help us to do Your will when we make up our minds

5. Our nations are going astray, please do not judge us

6. Revive Your Church and send Your repentance to the nations

7. Governments are adopting ungodly and secular policies, send Your fears into our socio-political leaders.

8. Some governments are becoming blatantly anti-Christ and anti-gospel, O LORD, please resist them from above

9. Some local, state and even national governments are sponsoring anti-christian terrorist groups. Please look down, deride and distress them to come back to their senses

10. Help us to widely spread the understanding that the primary responsibility of political governments is fear of God, justice and equity to provide a conducive atmosphere for the spread of the gospel and liberty for individuals' responses.

11. Thank You, LORD, for the few nations where leaders are defending the democratic liberty of the Church to preach the gospel. Let the number of such nations increase.

12. In this context we pray for President Trump and Prime Minister Boris Johnson of USA and UK respectively.

13. There are reports that our President has called on all

Africans, especially from the islamic world to come into our country without any immigration control. Please raise up people in his government who will convince him to review.

14. We pray for all nations where citizens of islamic countries are trooping into. Please use the arrangement to expose many muslims to the gospel and save the souls of many.

15. There was an attempt to establish RUGA settlements all over our country in the recent past. O LORD overrule in the matter.

16. However, where there are RUGA settlements send Your Spirit by Your Church to turn the settlements into evangelism fields and save the souls of many.

17. The arrangement to fulanise and/or islamize our nation will always fail.

18. The call of our nation's CJN for more of sharia in our constitution will spark off debates that will lead to the removal of sharia provisions from our national constitution.

19. We decree that a new religiously neutral constitution will soon be written for our nation.

20. The LORD will raise political leaders that fear Him and are committed to justice, equity and prosperity of the polity in our nation.

21. Our nation will prosper socially and economically in the gospel.

Knowing more about
CHRISFO

A. INTRODUCTION

Christian Foundations (CHRISFO) is a non-denominational platform of collaboration with churches and hristian fellowships, organizations, etc. with a ᴄvision for the revival of genuine New Testament Christianity in the hurch and the fear of God in the land.

B. ACTIVITIES

Our activities are as follows:

1. Solemn Assembly:

A program aimed to encourage effective prayers with fasting for the well being of our nation and compatriots. This includes;

a. Solemn Assembly Conference; a period of about three days of anointed biblical expositions and teachings for the revival of New Testament Christianity. This may include tours.

b. National Prayer Meetings; arranging special prayer meetings, tours, etc. in response to unique developments in the nation or any part of it.

2.   CHRISFO Affiliation

CHRISFO wants to work closely with you for the revival of New Testament Christianity and the fear of God in our land. Get in touch with us to collaborate.

C.   STUDY MATERIALS:

1.   CHRISFO STUDY OUTLINES (CSO):

Provide effective materials for Sunday School Outlines, House Fellowships, Bible Studies and other group and practical Bible discussions.

2.   CHRISFO CDs: Seek to spread the effects of the Holy Spirit in the CHRISFO messages on the principles of genuine New Testament Christianity.

3.   CHRISFO BOOKS:

Seek to present biblical expositions on the fundamental principles of genuine new testament Christianity.

4.   CHRISFO Tracts: are available for your distribution during evangelism, teachings and other gospel promotional endeavours.

D. CHRISFO BIBLE SCHOOL

The CHRSIFO Bible School is a platform of raising New Testament Christian ministers, who are approved unto

God and rightly dividing the Word of Truth.

E. CHINESE MINISTRY

We believe that the LORD has called CHRISFO to join in the evangelisation of Chinese people from different Asian countries that come into Africa. To facilitate this, CHRISFO has adopted a four action plan as follows:

1. Raising prayer guard among ministers across denominations, who have a burden for the salvation of Chinese people.

2. Giving the learning of Chinese language a prominent place in the CHRISFO Bible School.

3. Seeking for and appropriating opportunities to use Chinese Language to preach the gospel

4. Building Chinese Christian fellowships.

Contact us at:

SALVATION HOUSE,
1-3, Salvation Street, Off Pipeline Road,
Baale Akinosi, Ajuwon- Akute,
(via Ojodu Berger, Lagos)
Tel: 080 33011 351
E-mail: christianfoundations88@yahoo.com
web: www.chrisfo.org

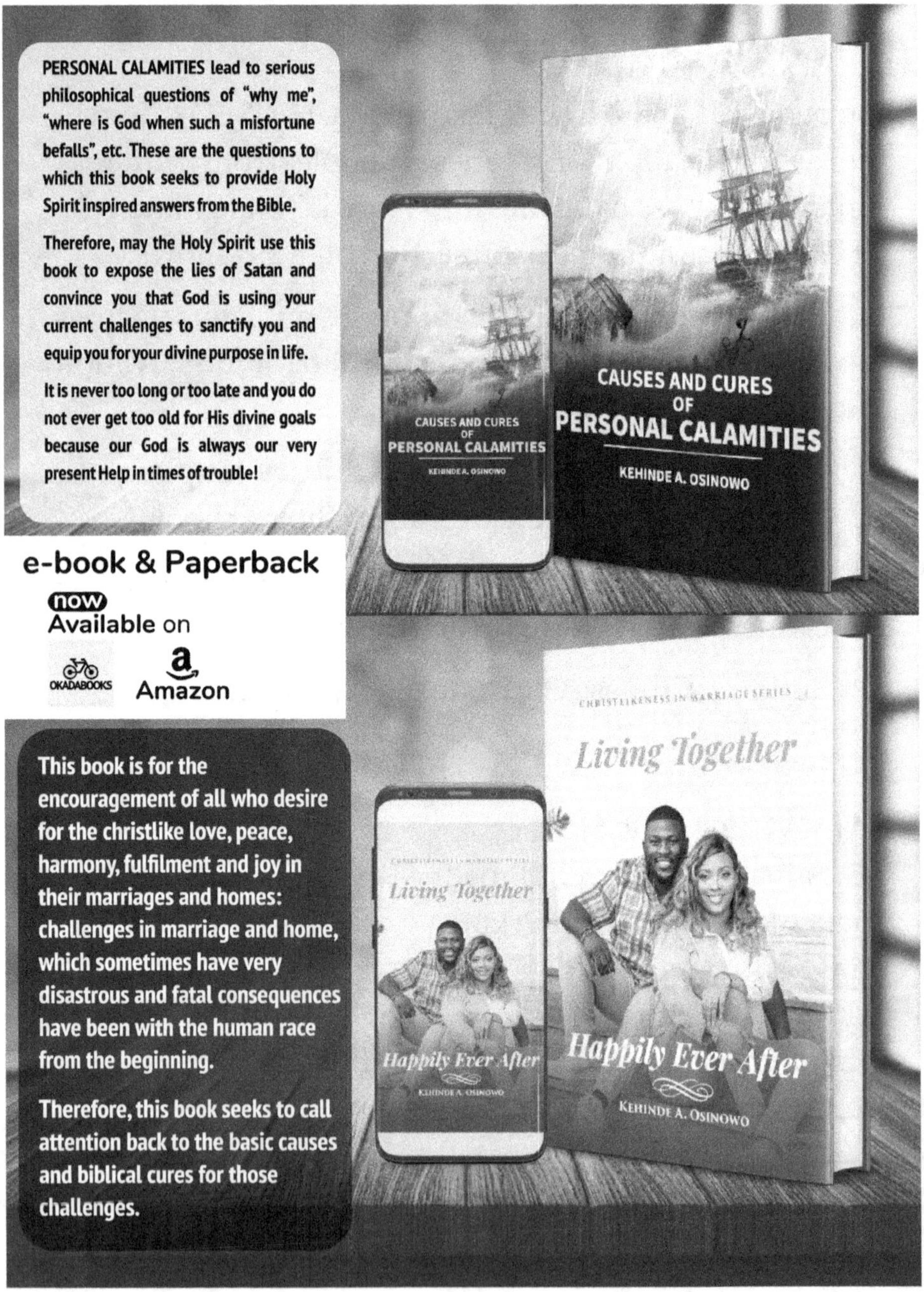

PERSONAL CALAMITIES lead to serious philosophical questions of "why me", "where is God when such a misfortune befalls", etc. These are the questions to which this book seeks to provide Holy Spirit inspired answers from the Bible.

Therefore, may the Holy Spirit use this book to expose the lies of Satan and convince you that God is using your current challenges to sanctify you and equip you for your divine purpose in life.

It is never too long or too late and you do not ever get too old for His divine goals because our God is always our very present Help in times of trouble!

e-book & Paperback

now Available on

This book is for the encouragement of all who desire for the christlike love, peace, harmony, fulfilment and joy in their marriages and homes: challenges in marriage and home, which sometimes have very disastrous and fatal consequences have been with the human race from the beginning.

Therefore, this book seeks to call attention back to the basic causes and biblical cures for those challenges.